now you're cookin'
SHRIMP

REBO
PUBLISHERS

Foreword

The oceans, rivers and lakes have provided us with an abundance of fish, crustaceans and shellfish since time immemorial. Fish are generally considered to be tasty and healthy because of their high protein, mineral and vitamin content, without saturated fats. Shrimp are one of the most popular shellfish. There are many types, including king shrimp, Dutch and Norwegian shrimp, and the more "exotic" shrimp such as Mexican and black tiger shrimp. Shrimp are primarily sold pre-cooked in the U.S. They can be eaten cold or can be heated in all sorts of ways — the possibilities are endless.

This book offers a wide variety of recipes with surprising combinations such as *Baked Mushrooms Filled with Shrimp*, *Braised Mushrooms with Chinese Vegetables* and *Pizza with Shrimp and Pepper*. These exciting recipes are sure to expand your repertoire!

Abbreviations

All measurements conform to European and American measurement systems. For easier cooking, the American cup measurement is used throughout the book.

tbsp = tablespoon

tsp = teaspoon

oz = ounce

lb = pound

°F = degrees Fahrenheit

°C = degrees Celsius

g = gram

kg = kilogram

cm = centimeter

ml = mililiter

l = liter

Butterfly

This method is often applied to raw shrimp for a more attractive and larger appearance. Cut the peeled shrimp almost completely through over its entire length. The traditional manner is to cut along the stomach. You can also make an incision along the back of the shrimp to give it a round shape, making it appear larger.

Peel

Carefully grasp the head of the shrimp and detach it from the body. With your fingers, remove the shell, keeping the legs intact. Start at the bottom. Exert slight pressure on the tail and carefully extract the meat. You can leave the shell of the tail on the body for a decorative effect.

Devein

Pull off the entire black intestinal vein with your fingers. For raw shrimp, it may be practical to use a knife to make a shallow slit in the back before you remove the intestinal vein.

Buy and store

Raw shrimp is available whole or peeled and without intestinal vein, both fresh and frozen. Cooked shrimp is available whole as well as peeled and without intestinal vein. Raw fish should have a firm body and succulent meat. The shell should be intact and fit around the body snugly.

Do not refreeze raw, defrosted shrimp. If you wish to consume the shrimp the same evening or on the day after purchase, all you have to do is remove from the plastic bag, place in a bowl, cover lightly, store in the coldest spot in the refrigerator. However, if you wish to consume the shrimp a couple of days later and you do not wish to freeze them, here are the best ways to keep them fresh:

Raw shrimp: place in a bowl with ice cubes, refreshing the ice cubes when they melt. Process the shrimp within two days.

Cooked shrimp: place in a bowl with ice cubes, refreshing the ice cubes when they melt. Shrimp left in water will lose their taste. Process the shrimp within two days.

Always leave shrimp in their shells to prevent them from drying out.

Freeze raw shrimp in a plastic container, making sure that they are immersed in water. Do not add salt. Cover the container and freeze. The water will form a block of ice that protects the shrimp from decay. Let the shrimp thaw for 24 hours in the refrigerator. Frozen shrimp can be kept for three months.

Nutritional information per 3½ oz/100 g

Calories	Protein (g)	Fat (g)	Cholesterol (mg)	Omega 3's (mg)
88 (raw)	20.5	0.6	149	212
103 (cooked)	23.5	0.9	188	N/A

Cooking times

Method of preparation	Size	Time
Steam	Medium large	10-15 minutes
	Medium small	5-10 minutes
Simmer	Large	5-6 minutes per kg
	Medium large	3-4 minutes per kg
	Small	2-3 minutes per kg
Deep-fry	Medium	2-4 minutes
Grill (all methods)	Medium	2-4 minutes
Microwave	per 4 oz in marinade	2 minutes

Tips and Information

Quality assessment

Judged by	Good quality	Poor quality
APPEARANCE		
Shell	Clean, intact	Damaged, weak appearance
Color	Clear, shiny	Dark edges around the body, the legs, shell, meat or intestinal area. Dry, faded parts
Head	Firm on the body	Loose on the body, discolored
SUBSTANCE		
Meat	Firm	Soft, slimy, granular
ODOR	Mild, hardly, perceptible	Mildly spoiled odor, a chemical or ammonia-like odor

Tip: soft and broken shells need not indicate poor quality. The shell may also be soft because it is newly acquired.

shrimp

Method

Heat the olive oil in a large saucepan and sauté the carrot, leek, and peppers for about 10 minutes. Add the paprika and the saffron, then sauté another few minutes.

Add the wine and bouillon and bring to a boil. Simmer for 15 minutes. Add the cubes of fish, the peeled shrimp, and the squid and simmer for another 5 minutes.

Ingredients

2 tbsp olive oil

2 large carrots, finely cut

3 leeks, cut into thin rings and washed thoroughly

1 red and 1 green pepper, chopped

1 tbsp paprika

a sizeable bunch saffron

2 cups white wine

3½ cups fish bouillon

1lb firm white fish fillets

1lb shrimp, peeled and deveined

1lb baby squid

2 tbsp finely chopped parsley,

1 lemon, cut into sections

Spanish Fish Soup with Saffron

shrimp

Method

To make the spicy sauce: Purée the tomatoes in a food processor and pour the mixture into a large bowl. Grind the pieces of yellow pepper and mix with the tomato. Add Tabasco and salt to taste. Refrigerate 1-8 hours. Cut the kernels of corn from the cob with a sharp knife. Toast the corn in a heavy skillet over high heat until lightly seared and golden brown. Transfer to a small bowl and set aside.

Wash the leek thoroughly and purée the white pieces, garlic, and the Bermuda onion in a food processor (or chop finely with a knife). Heat the oil in the skillet and add the finely chopped leek, Bermuda onion, garlic mixture and paprika and fry 5 minutes over medium heat until the vegetables are soft and evenly cooked.

Press the onion pieces against the side of the pan and add the shrimp. Sauté briefly until the shrimp turns pink on the bottom. Fry the other side. Mix the onion with the shrimp. Add the shrimp mixture to the cooled tomato mixture and mix together. Add half of the toasted corn, the lime juice, and the parsley, mixing everything together before returning to the refrigerator.

Divide the mixture between six martini or wine glasses, garnish with the coriander leaves and the remainder of the toasted corn, then serve.

Shrimp Gazpacho with Corn

Ingredients

4 large processed tomatoes, washed and halved

1 yellow pepper, seeded and quartered

¼ tsp Tabasco; ½ tsp salt; 2 corncobs

1 small leek, white part only, 1 clove garlic, peeled

1 small Bermuda onion; 1 tbsp olive oil; 1 tsp paprika

1 lb raw cocktail shrimp, peeled, with tail

juice from two limes; 2 tbsp fresh parsley, finely chopped

⅓ cup fresh coriander leaves, lemon sections for garnish

Method

Heat the oil in a saucepan over medium heat.

Add the onion and red pepper and sauté for about 5 minutes, stirring gently. Add the garlic and the ginger and sauté another 2 minutes.

Mix in the chicken broth and bring to a boil. Add the chicken, shrimp, Chinese noodles, bamboo shoots and mushrooms, reduce the heat and simmer 5 minutes until the noodles are ready.

Add the lettuce, scallions, coriander, soy sauce, and black pepper to taste. Mix well and serve immediately.

Ingredients

1 tbsp vegetable oil

1 onion, diced; 1 red pepper, cut

2 cloves garlic, pressed

½ tsp fresh ginger, finely cut

4 cups chicken broth

¼lb/125g chicken breast or chicken leg, cut into slices

20 small raw shrimp, peeled and deveined

4oz/125g rice vermicelli

4oz/125g can bamboo shoots, drained and cut

5 mushroom caps, sliced thinly

¼ head of lettuce, in strips; 2 scallions, chopped

2 tbsp fresh coriander, finely chopped; 1½ tbsp soy sauce

freshly ground black pepper

Shrimp-Chicken Soup

Method

Peel and devein the shrimp. Save the heads and shells. Heat the oil in a large saucepan. Add the shrimp heads and shells, then fry over high heat for 5 minutes, stirring, until the shells turn color. Mix in the galangal root or ginger, lemon leaves, lemon grass, halved peppers, and water. Cover the pan and bring to a boil. Simmer 15 minutes, stirring regularly.

Pour the liquid through a strainer into a clean saucepan. Discard the remaining ingredients. Add the shrimp to the cooking liquid and cook for 2 minutes. Add the coriander, pieces of pepper, and the lime juice and cook another minute until the shrimp is done. Ladle the soup into bowls and garnish with pieces of lime leaf.

Spicy Shrimp Soup

Ingredients

2lb/1kg medium-sized raw shrimp

1 tbsp vegetable oil

8 slices fresh or prepared galangal root or fresh ginger

8 kaffir lime leaves

2 sprigs fresh lemon grass, crushed or ½ tsp dried lemon grass, soaked in hot water until soft

2 fresh red Spanish peppers, halved and seeded

8 cups water

3 tbsp fresh coriander leaves

1 fresh red Spanish pepper, finely cut

2 tbsp lime juice

kaffir lime leaves, finely chopped

Method

Place the shrimp, onion, and tomato purée in a food processor and purée into a smooth paste.

Add the bouillon slowly while processing and wait until it thickens. Place the shrimp mixture in a saucepan and bring to a boil over low heat. Cook about 10 minutes, stirring regularly.

Add the cream, paprika, and black pepper to taste. Cook the soup for about 2 minutes.

Mix in the Sherry and serve immediately.

Ingredients

¾lb/315g cooked shrimp, peeled and deveined

½ onion, diced

4oz/125ml tomato purée

2½ cups chicken broth

⅓ cup heavy cream

⅛ tsp paprika

freshly ground black pepper

1-2 tbsp dry Sherry

Shrimp Bisque

Method

Mix olive oil, lemon juice, garlic, and celery seeds to form a thick dressing. Season to taste with pepper and salt. Set aside.

Bring bouillon to a boil and mix in the turmeric powder and cumin. Add the shrimp and squid, poaching them 2 minutes until the shrimp turns orange. Remove from the bouillon. Place the couscous in a large bowl. Pour over the remaining seasoned bouillon and mix well. Cover until the couscous absorbs the liquid, about 10 minutes.

Separate the couscous with a fork and add the shrimp and squid mixture, the tomato cubes, the celery, the scallions, and the mint leaf. Mix in the dressing.

Couscous with Seafood and Fresh Mint

Ingredients

½ cup olive oil

2½ cups fresh lemon juice

1 large garlic clove, finely chopped

1 tsp celery seed

salt and pepper to taste

⅛ tsp turmeric powder; ¼ tsp cumin

1½ cups vegetable bouillon

1lb/500g raw cocktail shrimp, peeled, with tail

½lb/200g small squid rings

¾lb/300g couscous

3 tomatoes, cut into small cubes

2 stalks celery, finely cut

6 scallions, finely chopped

20 fresh mint leaves, finely chopped

18

Method

Place the dried peaches on a flat plate. Mix lemon juice, grated lemon peel, brown sugar, salt, black pepper, sherry vinegar, and Tabasco together in a dish and pour the mixture over the peaches. Set aside at room temperature for 30 minutes.

Remove the peaches from the mixture. Place the mixture in a food processor, add the mustard and the egg and purée until smooth. Add the oil in a thin, steady trickle. The dressing is now creamy and somewhat thicker.

Distribute the mixed salad over four plates, placing two peach halves on each salad mound. Place three pieces of shrimp on each plate. Pour the dressing over the salad and serve immediately.

Ingredients

½lb/200g dried peaches

1 tbsp lemon juice; 1 tsp grated lemon peel

1 tsp brown sugar; ¼ tsp salt

¼ tsp freshly ground black pepper

3½ cups sherry vinegar

2 drops Tabasco

1lb/500g mixed salad

1 tsp Dijon mustard; 1 egg

⅔ cup light olive oil

12 cocktail shrimp, peeled and deveined

Peach and Shrimp Salad

Method

To make the dressing: Mix together the lemon juice, vinegar, and mustard.

Beat with a whisk while gradually adding the oil. Continue stirring until

the ingredients are creamy.

Place the water chestnuts, ginger, pineapple and shrimp in a bowl.

Add the dressing and carefully mix it in.

Distribute the salad over salad plates. Garnish with scallions and sesame seeds.

Shrimp and Pineapple Salad

Ingredients

1 tbsp fresh lemon juice

2 tbsp white wine vinegar

1 tbsp Dijon mustard

¼ cup olive oil

2 tbsp Oriental sesame oil

10 water chestnuts, drained and sliced

1 tbsp grated, fresh ginger

4oz/225g canned pineapple slices, drained
and cut into pieces

1lb/500g cooked shrimp, peeled

accompanying salad

3 scallions, cut into rings

1 tbsp sesame seeds, lightly roasted

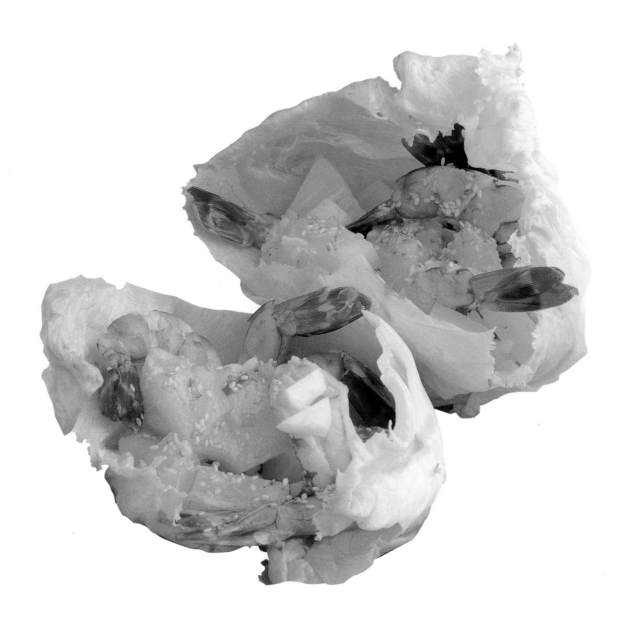

shrimp

Method

Cut the heads of the squid just under the eye.

Wash well and place in a pan of boiling water.

Cook until opaque, drain, and rinse under cold water.

Cut into small pieces.

Make the dressing, pour it over the squid, and marinate overnight.

Peel and devein the shrimp and mix with the squid. Cut the

avocados in half and remove the pits. Distribute the seafood over

the avocado halves and garnish with lemon slices and oregano.

Ingredients

6 mini squid

1lb/500g shrimp

3 ripe avocados

Dressing:

⅓ cup olive oil

2 tbsp lemon juice

1 hard-boiled egg, finely cut

1 tbsp fresh oregano, finely chopped

2 cloves garlic, pressed

Avocado with Seafood

Method

Peel and devein the shrimp.

Place the shrimp, avocado, and grapefruit on a plate. Prepare a dressing by mixing mayonnaise, sour cream, yogurt, and mint and pour it over the salad.

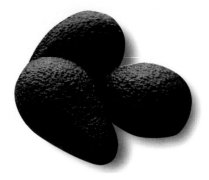

Avocado and Shrimp Salad

Ingredients

1½ lb/750g cooked cocktail shrimp

1 avocado, in slices

1 grapefruit

shrimp

27

Method

Place the squid rings on paper towel and dry.

Heat the oil in a skillet, add the shrimp and garlic and stir-fry 2 minutes over medium heat. Add the squid and stir-fry another 2 minutes. Set aside and cool.

Place the spinach, onion, pepper, peas, mint, and nuts in a bowl or on a plate. Distribute the seafood on top.

Prepare the dressing by mixing chili sauce, soy sauce, lime juice and oil in a bowl.

Pour the dressing over the salad and cool.

Ingredients

¾lb/375g squid rings

1 tbsp olive oil

¾lb/375g medium-sized raw shrimp, peeled and deveined

1 clove garlic, pressed; 1lb/500g spinach

1 red onion, cut in rings

1 red pepper, cut in strips

9oz/250g (snow) peas, cleaned

2 tbsp fresh mint leaves

1oz/30g nuts, finely chopped

Chili dressing:

2 tbsp sweet chili sauce; 1 tbsp soy sauce

1 tbsp lime juice; 1 tbsp vegetable oil

Seafood Salad

shrimp

Method

Prepare the marinade by mixing the black pepper, chili sauce, soy sauce, garlic, and lemon juice in a bowl. Add the shrimp, making sure they are evenly covered with the marinade and set the covered bowl aside 1 hour. Turn the shrimp regularly. Prepare the mango cream by placing the pulp and the coconut milk in a food processor. Puree until smooth. Prepare a moderately hot barbecue. Place the shrimp on the barbecue, and bake 3-4 minutes until they turn color. Serve with mango cream.

Note: coconut milk is available in various forms: canned, in cardboard containers or in powder form to be diluted with water. Once opened, the milk is only good for a number of days. Coconut milk is available in Asian specialty stores and in some supermarkets. However, you can also easily make coconut milk yourself. Place 1 lb dried coconut in a bowl and add 1/3 cup of boiling water. Let the bowl stand for half an hour and drain the coconut. Squeeze out the coconut, removing as much liquid as possible. This coconut milk is fairly thick. The coconut can be reused to make thinner milk.

Peppered Shrimp with Mango Cream

Ingredients

3½ lb/1¾ kg raw jumbo shrimp, peeled and deveined, with tail

Chili marinade:

1 tsp crushed black pepper

1 tbsp sweet chili sauce; 1 tbsp soy sauce

1 clove garlic, pressed; ¼ cup lemon juice

Mango cream:

1 mango, peeled, pitted, and cut coarsely; 3 tbsp coconut milk

shrimp

Method

Prepare the marinade and mix together all ingredients, except the shrimp. Peel and devein the shrimp, but leave the tail. Place the shrimp in a glass bowl and cover with marinade. Cover the bowl and refrigerate for 1 hour. String the shrimp on the skewers horizontally or vertically.

Prepare a moderately hot barbecue. Cover the grill with aluminum foil and place the shrimp on top. Bake 4-5 minutes on each side: they will turn pink. Coat with marinade while barbecuing. Place the shrimp on a plate, remove from the skewers, and serve immediately.

Shrimp with Honey and Cayenne Pepper

Ingredients

1lb/500g raw cocktail shrimp

¼ cup red wine

½ cup honey

⅛ tsp cayenne pepper

½ tsp mustard powder

wooden skewers, soaked

shrimp

Method

Blanch the onions until they are nearly done, drain, and rinse with cold water.

Remove the fatty edges from the bacon and cut each slice into three pieces.
Roll up each slice.

String the shrimp, scallops, and bacon on skewers and complete each skewer
with an onion.

Mix oil, butter, dill, parsley, scallions, garlic, pepper, lemon rasp, and lemon juice.

Dip the skewers in mixture and let them stand for an hour.

Remove the skewers from the marinade and bake them on a preheated
barbecue until done. Cover them regularly with the marinade.

Kebabs with Shrimp and Scallops

Ingredients

1lb/500g raw shrimp, peeled and deveined, with tail

¾ lb/400g scallops

½ lb/250g onions; 6 slices of bacon

2 tbsp olive oil; 4 tbsp butter

2 tbsp fresh dill, finely chopped; 2 tbsp parsley, finely chopped

2 scallions, diced; 2 cloves garlic, pressed

freshly ground black pepper; 2 tbsp lemon juice; 1 tsp grated lemon peel

shrimp

Method

Mix oil, curry paste, ginger, garlic, lime juice, and yogurt in a bowl.

Add the shrimp, mixing through to cover with the mixture.

Cover the bowl and marinate for 2-3 hours in the refrigerator.

Drain the shrimp and string three on a greased skewer. Do the same with the rest of the shrimp until you have twelve kebabs. Roll the kebabs through the sesame seeds and bake evenly on a lightly greased, preheated barbecue or grill for 3 minutes until the shrimp is done.

Prepare the masala onions. Melt the ghee or butter over medium heat in a saucepan. Add the onions and sauté 5 minutes, stirring until they become soft. Add the masala curry. Cook until piping hot, about 2 minutes. Serve with the shrimp.

Ingredients

1 tbsp vegetable oil; 1 tbsp madras curry paste

2 tbsp fresh ginger, finely ground

2 cloves garlic, pressed

2 tbsp lemon juice; ½ cup plain yogurt

36 medium-sized raw shrimp with tail, unpeeled and deveined

6 tbsp sesame seeds, roasted

Green masala onions:

2 tbsp ghee or butter

2 onions, cut in sections; 2 tbsp green masala curry

Spicy Shrimp Kebabs with Sesame Seeds

Method

To make the marinade: Mix all ingredients and allow the mixture to stand for 1 hour.

Peel the shrimp, leaving the tail intact. Place in a non-metallic bowl and cover with the marinade. Cover the bowl and refrigerate for 1-2 hours. String the shrimp on the skewers (2-3 small shrimp per skewer or 1 cocktail shrimp with the tail on top).

Light the barbecue and place a square piece of baking paper on the grill. Place the shrimp on top and cover both sides with marinade while they grill. Grill the shrimp until they turn pink. Do not overcook.

Shrimp Teriyaki

Ingredients

2lb/1kg fresh, raw shrimp, unpeeled

Teriyaki marinade:

½ cup soy sauce; 2 tbsp brown sugar

¼ tsp ground ginger

2 tbsp wine vinegar

1 clove garlic, pressed; 2 tbsp tomato puree

wooden skewers, soaked

Method

Place the shrimp along with the lime juice, garlic, ginger and sugar in a medium-sized bowl and mix well. Cover and refrigerate for 30 minutes.

Cut the bacon into 1in/2cm strips and wrap around each shrimp. String two shrimp on each skewer. Grill them under a moderately hot grill 2 minutes on each side, until done.

Marinated Shrimp in Bacon

Ingredients

32 raw cocktail shrimp, peeled and deveined

¼ cup fresh lime juice

1 clove garlic, pressed

1 tbsp grated ginger

2 tbsp brown sugar

16 slices of bacon, without rind

Method

Peel and devein the shrimp. Leave tail attached.

Mix the oil, wine, scallions, lemon juice, and pepper.

String the shrimp on the skewers (approximately three per skewer).

Place the skewers in a shallow bowl and pour over the marinade.

Marinate for at least 1 hour.

Roll the shrimp with the roasted sesame seeds.

Refrigerate for another 30 minutes before cooking.

Fry the shrimp on the griddle or a very hot barbecue,

2 minutes on each side.

Cover while frying with the marinade.

Ingredients

2lb/1kg medium-sized cocktail shrimp

¼ cup olive oil

¼ cup red wine

4 scallions, diced

½ tsp grated lemon peel

¼ tsp crushed black peppercorns

12 wooden skewers (soaked in water 30 minutes)

4oz/125g roasted sesame seeds

Barbecued Shrimp with Sesame Seeds

shrimp

Method

Place the coconut milk, shrimp paste, curry paste, lemon grass, peppers, cumin, and coriander in a wok and bring everything to a slow boil over medium heat.

Simmer 10 minutes and stir occasionally.

Mix the shrimp, cucumber, bamboo shoots, and tamarind through the coconut milk mixture and cook, stirring regularly, another 10 minutes, until the shrimp is done.

Sour Shrimp Curry

Ingredients

2 cups coconut milk; ½ tsp shrimp paste

2 tbsp Thai green curry paste, 1 sprig fresh lemon grass, finely chopped

or ¼ tsp dried lemon grass, soaked in hot water until soft

2 fresh green bell peppers, finely cut

1 tbsp ground cumin; 1 tbsp ground coriander

1lb/500g large, raw shrimp, peeled and deveined

3 cucumbers, halved and sliced

5oz/125g canned bamboo shoots, drained

1 tbsp tamarind concentrate, dissolved in 3 tbsp hot water

shrimp

Method

Grind the lemon grass, scallions, garlic, peppers, turmeric powder, and the coriander in a food processor.

Heat the oil in a wok and add the shrimp paste.

Fry for 1 minute and add the shrimp paste with the thin part of the coconut milk.

Add the shrimp and the rest of the coconut milk as soon as the mixture begins to boil.

Heat for a couple of minutes and mix in the drained pineapple slices. Simmer another 10 minutes. Serve with steamed rice.

Ingredients

1lb/500g raw cocktail shrimp, peeled and deveined

1 sprig lemon grass, coarsely removed

5 scallions, peeled

3 cloves garlic, peeled

4 fresh red bell peppers, halved and seeded

½ tsp ground turmeric powder; 3 tbsp coriander, finely chopped

6 tbsp vegetable oil; ¼ tsp shrimp paste

1 can coconut milk; 1 can pineapple slices

salt to taste

Pineapple-Shrimp Curry

Method

Marinate the shrimp, half of the sprigs of coriander, the garlic, the salt, and the lemon juice in the oil for a number of hours.

To make the sauce: add the wine, vermouth, wine vinegar, and scallions to the marinade. Bring to a boil and let thicken until only about 3 tablespoons remain. Add blocks of butter over low heat, stirring with a whisk until the sauce becomes thick. Flavor with a little lemon juice, salt, and pepper. Chop the rest of the coriander and stir it through the butter sauce.

Heat a large skillet and fry the shrimp in it for about 2 minutes. Make sure that a pan of salted, boiling water is ready. Cook the peas, the red pepper, and the mushrooms for about 1 minute.

Drain the vegetables and add to the shrimp in the skillet. Distribute the shrimp mixture between four plates. Heat the sauce and pour it over the shrimp mixture.

Shrimp with Coriander Butter

Ingredients

1½ lb/750g large cocktail shrimp with tail, peeled and deveined

¼ cup olive oil

1 bunch coriander

2 cloves garlic, pressed

salt to taste

2 tbsp lemon juice

¼ cup dry white wine

¼ cup dry vermouth

1 tbsp white wine vinegar

2 tbsp scallions, diced

3oz/90g butter

9oz/250g (snow) peas

½ red pepper, cut into thin strips

4oz/125g Oriental mushrooms or mushroom caps

Method

Place the noodles in a bowl of boiling water and let stand for 5 minutes. Drain and set aside.

Heat the vegetable oil in a wok over medium heat, add the eggs, and tilt the wok so that the bottom and sides are covered with egg. Bake another 2 minutes until they set. Remove the omelet from the wok, let it cool, roll it up, and cut into thin strips.

Heat the sesame oil in a clean wok and add onion, red pepper, garlic and peppers.

Stir-fry over high heat for 3 minutes. Add the shrimp and the pork, then stir-fry another 3 minutes.

Place the noodles, strips of egg, scallions, coriander, sugar, turmeric powder, cumin, and soy sauce in the wok and stir-fry another 3 minutes until well-heated.

Ingredients

1lb/500g fresh noodles

1 tsp vegetable oil; 2 eggs, slightly beaten

½ tsp sesame oil; 1 onion, diced

1 red pepper, sliced; 2 cloves garlic, pressed

1 fresh red Spanish pepper

8 raw jumbo shrimp, peeled and deveined

½lb/250g barbecued or roasted Chinese pork, cut into thin slices

6 scallions, in rings; 2 tbsp fresh coriander leaves

½ tsp sugar; ½ tsp ground turmeric powder

¼ tsp ground cumin; 2 tbsp soy sauce

Singapore Noodles

Method

Mix the shrimp with the wine, cornstarch, and soy sauce in a bowl. Cover the bowl and let it cool for at least half an hour.

Heat 4 tablespoons of oil in a wok and fry the shrimp until they turn pink. Remove the shrimp from the wok and add the remainder of the oil. Sauté the shrimp in the oil for 2 minutes. Return the shrimp to the wok and add the seasoning. Shake until well-heated and serve immediately.

Braised Shrimp with Chinese Vegetables

Ingredients

1½ lbs/750g raw shrimp, peeled and deveined

1 tbsp Chinese wine or dry sherry

½ tsp cornstarch; ½ tsp soy sauce

12 snow peas

1 box snow peas or Chinese cabbage, 5 tbsp oil

Seasoning:

¼ tsp sugar

1 tsp soy sauce

½ tsp sesame oil

¼ tsp salt

shrimp

Method

Place the garlic, coriander and 2 tablespoons of oil in a food processor
and grind until smooth.

Heat the remainder of the oil in a large wok or skillet, add the garlic mixture,
and stir-fry for 2 minutes. Add the shrimp and cover, stirring with the garlic
mixture.

Mix in water, fish sauce, sugar, and black pepper to taste
and stir-fry until the shrimp is done.

Thai Garlic Shrimp

Ingredients

6 cloves garlic, pressed

5 tbsp fresh coriander, finely chopped

3 tbsp vegetable oil

1 lb/500g raw jumbo shrimp with tail,

peeled and deveined

¾ cup water

¼ cup fish sauce

½ tsp sugar

freshly ground black pepper

Method

Butterfly the shrimp and dust with salt, pepper, and flour.

Dip in egg and let the excess egg drip off.

Sprinkle with a mixture of sesame seeds and coconut. Set aside.

Mix mango, onion, coriander, and lime juice in a bowl and season to taste with salt and pepper.

Heat the butter or olive oil in a skillet, add the cocktail shrimp and sauté on each side 1-2 minutes over high heat until golden brown.

Place some vegetables on each plate. Spoon three fried shrimp, top with a generous amount of mango salsa and serve.

Ingredients

12 raw cocktail shrimp with tail, peeled

salt and pepper, to taste

flour; 1 egg, beaten

4oz/125g sesame seeds, 3oz/90g coconut

1 mango, peeled and cut into small pieces

½ small Bermuda onion, diced

2 tbsp coriander, finely chopped; juice from 1 lime

2 tbsp butter or olive oil

various vegetables as desired

Cocktail Shrimp with Sesame, Coconut, and Mango Salsa

Method

Peel and devein the shrimp. Leave the tails intact. Make a vertical incision along the back of the shrimp. Cut down the middle approximately ½in/2cm.

Cut the ham, zucchini, and scallions into slices and press a strip through the opening of each shrimp. Heat the oil in a wok or skillet. Add the shrimp and stir-fry for 1 minute.

Mix the ingredients for the dip sauce in a wok or pan. Heat until the mixture boils and thickens. Use as dip sauce for the shrimp.

Butterfly Shrimp

Ingredients	For the dip sauce
1lb/500g raw cocktail shrimp	2 tbsp cornstarch, diluted with 2½ cups water
1 piece of ham	1 cube chicken bouillon; 2 tbsp sherry
1 zucchini	2 tbsp soy sauce; 2 tbsp ginger
6 scallions	1 clove garlic, pressed
2 tbsp vegetable oil	1 cup water

Method

Dip the shrimp in the egg white and roll through the coconut until covered.

Heat the vegetable oil in a saucepan.

(The oil is hot enough if a piece of bread turns brown after 50 seconds.)

Fry the shrimp until golden brown and crispy in small portions for
2-3 minutes. Drain on paper towel and keep warm.

Heat the sesame oil in a wok over high heat and add the red and green
pepper slivers, garlic, ginger root, and kaffir lime leaves. Stir-fry
2-3 minutes until the aroma emerges.

Place the scallops in the wok and stir-fry until opaque about 3 minutes.
Add the fried shrimp, the peas or sprouts, sugar, lime juice, and fish sauce,
then stir-fry 2 minutes until warm.

Ingredients

2lb/1kg raw jumbo shrimp with tail, peeled and deveined

3 egg whites, lightly beaten; 3oz/900g grated coconut

vegetable frying fat, 1 tbsp sesame oil

4 fresh Spanish red peppers, seeded and finely cut

2 small fresh green Spanish peppers, seeded and finely cut

2 cloves garlic, pressed; 1 tbsp fresh ginger root, grated

3 kaffir lime leaves, finely chopped

¾lb/375g scallops, 4oz/125g snow peas or sprouts

2 tbsp palm sugar or brown sugar; ¼ cup lime juice

2 tbsp Thai fish sauce (ram pla)

Coconut Shrimp and Scallops

Method

To make the batter: mix the rice flour, salt, pepper, sugar, coconut milk, and turmeric powder until smooth. Wash, dry, and chop the shrimp coarsely. Wash the bean sprouts and set aside.

Cut the pork or the chicken into cubes. Heat a large skillet and pour in some oil.

Add the meat, onion, and shrimp and fry, stirring, until the shrimp changes color and the meat is done. Pour enough batter in the pan to cover all ingredients.

Place some bean sprouts on top and cover the pan. Fry 2 minutes until crispy. Turn and fry the other side until golden brown. Prepare the dressing by mixing together all the ingredients. Place a Vietnamese mint leaf on a piece of crepe. Roll in an iceberg lettuce leaf and sprinkle with some dressing. Serve immediately.

Tip: you can also make vegetarian crepes by replacing the meat and the shrimp with 1 medium-sized carrot and half a medium-sized red pepper (both cut into thin strips). Then proceed as above.

Vietnamese Crepes with Dip Sauce

Ingredients

½lb/250g rice flour; ½ tsp salt

1 tsp sugar

1 cup canned coconut milk; 1 cup water

¼ tsp ground turmeric powder

½lb cocktail shrimp, peeled

7oz/200g bean sprouts

¼lb/100g pork or chicken filet

1 onion, diced; sesame oil (used to fry)

For the dressing

1½ tsp fish sauce

2½ tsp sugar; 2 tbsp water

1 small red Spanish pepper, finely chopped

1 clove garlic, pressed

Vietnamese mint leaves, as garnish

Iceberg lettuce leaves, as garnish

Method

Place the pizza crust on a lightly greased baking sheet, cover with tomato purée and set aside.

Heat the oil in a skillet. Add the cumin, peppers, and garlic and sauté, stirring, for 1 minute. Mix in the lemon juice and the shrimp and sauté another 3 minutes until the shrimp turns color and is nearly done.

Cover the pizza crust with the red and yellow or green pepper strips. Cover with the shrimp mixture and add coriander, Parmesan cheese, and black pepper to taste.

Bake the pizza 20 minutes until the crust is crispy and golden brown.

Pizza with Shrimp and Pepper

Ingredients

1 frozen pizza crust

3 tbsp tomato purée, 1 tsp vegetable oil

½ tsp ground cumin

3 fresh red Spanish peppers, seeded and finely cut

2 cloves garlic, pressed; 2 tbsp lemon juice

1lb/500g raw shrimp, peeled and deveined

1 red pepper, cut; 1 yellow or green pepper, cut

2 tbsp fresh coriander, finely chopped; 2 tbsp grated Parmesan cheese

freshly ground black pepper

Method

Place the tamarind pulp and the water in a bowl and let stand for 20 minutes. Drain, save the liquid, and set aside. Discard the hard pieces.

Heat the oil in a wok or skillet. Add the Spanish peppers, the lemon grass, or the grated peel and stir-fry for 1 minute. Add the shrimp and stir-fry for another 2 minutes until the shrimp turns color.

Add mangos, coriander, sugar, lime juice, and tamarind liquid and stir-fry for another 5 minutes.

Ingredients

2 tbsp tamarind pulp, ½ cup water

1 tsp vegetable oil

3 sprigs fresh lemon grass, finely chopped or 1 tsp grated lemon peel

2 fresh red Spanish peppers, cut

1lb/500g medium-sized raw shrimp with tail, peeled and deveined

2 green (unripe) mangos, peeled and cut into thin slices

3 tbsp fresh coriander leaves, finely chopped

2 tbsp brown sugar; 2 tbsp lime juice

Stir-fried Tamarind Shrimp

shrimp

Method

Heat 2 tablespoons of oil in a saucepan and sauté the onion. Add

the red pepper, the garlic, and the tomatoes and sauté for 7 minutes.

Add the spinach, the white wine, the lemon juice, and the salt and pepper.

Cover the pan and simmer 8-10 minutes (until the spinach is done).

Remove the pan from the heat, mix well, and keep warm.

Place the rest of the oil in a large skillet. Add the shrimp when

the oil is hot, and sauté, stirring constantly until done (about 3 minutes).

Add the shrimp to the spinach and mix well.

Place in a warm serving dish and garnish with lemon wedges.

Ingredients

½ cup olive oil; 1 onion, diced

1 red pepper, seeded and cut

1 clove garlic, pressed

2 tomatoes, skinned and cut into pieces

1-1½ bunchfresh spinach, washed and cut coarsely

2 tbsp dry, white wine, juice from 1 lemon

salt and freshly ground black pepper

1lb/250g raw shrimp, peeled and deveined

lemon wedges as garnish

Shrimp with Spinach

Method

Heat the oil in a skillet. Add the shrimp and sauté over medium heat, one minute on each side. Remove the shrimp with a slotted spoon and set aside. Add tomato paste, sugar, garlic, chili sauce, and coriander to the frying fat and fry 1 minute.

Return the shrimp to the pan, add the sun-dried tomatoes and mix in the chili sauce. Sprinkle with lime juice. Place the shrimp on a serving plate. Garnish with young peas.

Spicy Shrimp with Sun-dried Tomatoes

Ingredients

3 tbsp olive oil

2lb/1kg raw cocktail shrimp with tail, peeled and deveined

1 tbsp tomato purée; 1 tsp brown sugar

2 cloves garlic, pressed; 1 tbsp chili sauce

1 tbsp coriander, finely chopped

6oz/180g sun-dried tomatoes, drained

1 tbsp fresh lime juice

young peas for garnish

shrimp

Method

Place the shrimp, garlic, olive oil, pepper, and rosemary in a large bowl and mix well. Place the bowl covered in the refrigerator and marinate for 8 hours or overnight. Melt the butter over high heat in a large skillet, add the shrimp, and sauté approximately 2 minutes until they turn pink.

Scoop the shrimp into a bowl with a slotted spoon. Remove the sprigs of rosemary. Pour the vermouth into the skillet, bring to a boil, and let it thicken until syrupy. Add the shrimp and carefully fold into the sauce. Spoon into a dish and serve immediately.

Garlic and Rosemary Shrimp

Ingredients

1lb/500g raw shrimp, peeled and deveined

2 cloves garlic, pressed

3 tbsp olive oil

⅛ tsp ground black pepper

2 sprigs fresh rosemary

2 tbsp butter; ½ cup dry vermouth

shrimp

Method

Cook the pasta in a large pan of boiling water according to the package directions. Drain and set aside. Keep warm.

Prepare the sauce. Melt the butter in a saucepan over medium heat, mix in the flour, and let stand for 1 minute.

Remove the pan from the heat and mix in the milk, saffron, and sage, stirring with a whisk. Return the pan to the heat and bring the sauce to a boil, stirring 3-4 minutes until thickened.

Add the shrimp and peas to the warm pasta and mix through. Cover with sauce and serve immediately.

Ingredients

1lb/500g pasta

1lb/500g cooked shrimp, peeled and deveined

4oz/125g snow peas, blanched

Saffron sauce

2 tbsp butter

1 tbsp flour

1 cup 2% milk

½ tbsp thread saffron or a dash of saffron powder

1 tbsp fresh sage, finely chopped

or ¼ tsp dried sage

Pasta with Saffron and Shrimp

Method

Chop the shrimp coarsely and mix with the finely chopped scallions, the lemon grass, the ginger, the coriander, the fish sauce, and the sweet chili sauce. Marinate for 1 hour. Meanwhile, mash the sweet potatoes. Mix turmeric powder, coconut milk, water, self-rising flour, rice flour, and cornstarch in a separate bowl. Mix well and add the grated potatoes. Set aside until the shrimp is ready.

Add the shrimp mixture to the batter and mix well. Heat the sesame oil and add a couple of tablespoons of the shrimp mixture to a nonstick skillet. Fry over medium heat for 3 minutes until they are crispy and golden brown. Turn them over and fry the other side. Remove the beignets from the pan. Cool on a baking grill and serve with lemon wedges. If you wish to reheat the beignets, place the grill 5-10 minutes in the oven (preheated to 400°F/200°C).

Tip: you can also use fresh salmon instead of shrimp.
Cut the salmon into cubes and mix through the marinade.
Prepare the rest of the dish as described above.
A combination of both fish is also tasty.

Shrimp with a Sweet Potato Crust

Ingredients	For the batter
1lb/500g large, raw shrimp, peeled and deveined	¾ lb/380g sweet potatoes
2 scallions, finely chopped	¼ tsp turmeric powder
1 sprig lemon grass, finely chopped	1 cup coconut milk
1 tbsp fresh ginger, chopped	4 tbsp self-rising flour
½ bunch fresh coriander, finely chopped	½ cup water
½ tsp fish sauce; 1 tbsp chili sauce	4 tbsp rice flour
2 tbsp sesame oil	1 tbsp cornstarch

shrimp

Method

Cut the shrimp lengthwise along the back.

Mix the oil with the lemon juice, the garlic, the peppers,

and the parsley in a bowl.

Add the shrimp and stir through the mixture.

Marinate for 2-3 hours.

Heat the oil in a large pan, dredge the shrimp in the flour,

and deep fry 2-3 minutes in the oil.

Drain on paper towel.

Serve with lemon wedges and parsley.

Ingredients

2lb/1kg (approx. 20 pieces) raw shrimp with tail, peeled and deveined

2 tbsp olive oil

1 tbsp lemon juice

2 cloves garlic, pressed

2 red Spanish peppers, seeded and finely cut

2 tbsp parsley, finely chopped

4 tbsp flour

frying fat

lemon (for garnish)

Butterfly Shrimp with Garlic, Pepper, and Parsley

Method

Make the dough by mixing the flour and butter in a food processor until the mixture looks like coarse breadcrumbs. Add enough water, while the machine is still on, to make a smooth dough. Knead the dough another 3 minutes on a flour-dusted surface and make 12 portions. Cover with a moist towel and set aside.

Make the filling: Heat the oil in a skillet. Add the onion, oregano, and thyme and sauté 4 minutes until the onion is golden brown. Add the tomatoes, shrimp, and peppers and sauté another 5 minutes until the mixture thickens. Let it cool.

Roll out each portion of dough into a thin 7 in/18cm circle. Place three tablespoons of filling on half of the dough circle and fold, pressing the edges together. Heat the oil in a saucepan. The oil is hot enough if a cube of bread turns brown within 50 seconds. Deep-fry the empanadas (several at a time) 2-3 minutes until crispy and golden brown. Drain on paper towel.

Empanadas with Shrimp

Ingredients

vegetable frying fat; empanada dough

1½ cups flour; 4 tbsp soft butter

¾ cup warm water

1 tsp fresh lemon thyme leaves

1lb/500g raw shrimp, peeled

2 fresh tomatoes, skinned and cut

4 Spanish peppers, roasted, seeded, peeled, and cut into pieces

5 mushroom caps, cut into thin pieces

¼ head of lettuce cut into strips

2 scallions, cut into thin rings

Pepper-shrimp filling

1 tsp vegetable frying fat

1 onion, diced

1 tbsp fresh oregano leaves

80

shrimp

Method

Fry the strips of bacon in a skillet over medium heat until crispy, about 5 minutes. Remove from the pan and drain on paper towel.

Place the onion in the pan and sauté, stirring until soft, but not brown, about 5 minutes. Add paprika, celery, and garlic, then sauté another 3 minutes. Add the rice and sauté, stirring regularly until glazed, about 5 minutes.

Add the broth, tomatoes, seasoning, and thyme, and bring to a boil. Cover the pan, lower the heat and cook for 15 minutes. Mix in the shrimp and the ham, cover the pan and cook another 10 minutes, until the rice is done and the liquid is absorbed.

Sprinkle the scallions on top and serve immediately.

Ingredients

3 slices bacon, cut into strips

1 large onion, diced; 1 green pepper, cut

1 celery stalk, sliced; 3 cloves garlic, pressed

1 cup long-grain rice

1½-2 cups chicken broth

2 cups strained canned tomatoes, pureed

1 tsp Cajun seasoning; ½ tsp dried thyme

1lb/500g raw, medium-sized shrimp, peeled and deveined

¼ lb/155g piece cooked ham, cut into cubes

3 scallions, diced

Jambalaya with Shrimp

Method

Heat the oil in a large, heavy skillet and sauté the shrimp, the green pepper, and the celery for several minutes until they become soft. Add the cut tomato, fish bouillon, salt, pepper, cayenne pepper, and the bouquet garni. Bring to a boil and simmer about 25 minutes.

Remove the vegetables from the pan and set aside. Reduce the liquid in the pan by half and cook over medium heat. Return the vegetables with the shrimp to the pan.

Simmer another 5 minutes. Remove the bouquet garni and sprinkle with finely chopped parsley before serving.

Creole Shrimp

Ingredients

¼ cup olive oil

1 large onion, finely diced

1 green pepper; 1 large celery stalk

4 large ripe tomatoes, skinned and cut

2 cups fish bouillon (or shrimp bouillon, drawn from shrimp heads and shells)

salt and freshly ground black pepper

a dash of cayenne pepper; 1 bouquet garni

2lb/1kg raw shrimp, peeled; parsley, finely chopped

Method

Make the marinade by mixing chili powder, oregano, garlic, grated orange, and lime peel in a bowl. Add the shrimp and mix.

Marinate in a covered bowl in the refrigerator for one hour.

Drain the shrimp and sauté on both sides on a pre-heated coal grill or barbecue grill until they turn color (about 1 minute).

Mix the papaya and the mint in a bowl. Spoon the shrimp on the plates, distribute the papaya mixture on top, place the lime wedges and finely cut peppers alongside, and serve.

Ingredients

2lb/1kg medium-sized raw shrimp, unpeeled

9oz/400g papaya, cut into pieces

2 tbsp fresh mint, finely chopped, lime wedges

Spanish peppers, cut

Orange marinade:

2 tbsp mild chili powder

2 tbsp fresh oregano, finely chopped

2 cloves garlic, pressed

1 tsp grated orange peel

1 tsp grated lime peel

¼ cup orange juice; ¼ cup lime juice

Barbecued Shrimp with Spanish Pepper

Method

Steam or microwave the peas, broccoli, and asparagus separately or cook in the microwave. Drain and rinse under cold running water. Set aside.

Pour the bouillon in a large saucepan and bring to a boil. Add the shrimp, fish, and scallops to the bouillon and cook 5 minutes until done. Remove with a slotted spoon and set aside.

Mix the cream, tomato puree and tarragon into the bouillon and bring to a boil. Temper the heat and simmer 10 minutes until the liquid is reduced by a third.

Add the remaining vegetables and seafood to the sauce and cook 1-2 minutes until piping hot. Season with black pepper and serve immediately.

Seafood with Green Vegetables

Ingredients

4oz/100g snow peas

4oz/100g broccoli flowerets

9oz/400g asparagus, cleaned

1⅔ cups fish bouillon

½lb/250g large raw shrimp, peeled and deveined, with tail

½lb/250g firm white fish fillets, cut into 3/4 inch cubes

½lb/250g scallops

½ cup heavy cream

4 tbsp tomato puree

1 tbsp fresh tarragon, finely chopped

or ½ tsp dried tarragon

freshly ground black pepper

Method

Heat the oil in a skillet over medium heat. Sauté the carrot, celery, and leek or onion, stirring, until they are crispy. Remove the vegetables from the pan with a slotted spoon and place them on a plate. Add the mushrooms and sauté both sides, while stirring, for 1 minute. Distribute the mushrooms over a casserole dish. Preheat the oven to 350°F/170°C.

Melt the butter in a skillet over medium heat.

Add the shrimp and the garlic and sauté, stirring until they become pink. Add the parsley and the lemon juice, then season with pepper and salt. Cook while stirring. Remove the pan from the heat. Reserve some shrimp for garnish.

Cut the rest of the shrimp into small pieces, distribute over the mushroom caps and bake 4-6 minutes in the oven until piping hot. Return the vegetables to the skillet, season with black pepper and salt and heat.

Place two mushrooms on each preheated plate. Add the vegetables, garnish with the remaining shrimp and serve.

Tip: Garlic is excellent with this hearty dish.

Ingredients

4 tbsp vegetable oil

1 small carrot, cut into thin strips

1 celery stalk, cut into thin strips

½ leek or onion, cut into thin strips

8 large, open mushrooms, without stems, 4oz/125g butter

1lb/500g raw shrimp with tail, peeled and deveined

5 cloves garlic, pressed; salt; freshly ground black pepper

4 tbsp fresh parsley, finely chopped; 3 tbsp fresh lemon juice

Baked Mushrooms Filled with Shrimp

Method

Marinate the shrimp for at least six hours (or overnight) in a mixture of the lemon juice, pepper, garlic, and sugar. The acid in the marinade will "cook the shrimp cold." The shrimp should turn a pinkish color when ready.

Remove the shrimp from the marinade and mix with the remaining ingredients.

Add salt and pepper to taste.

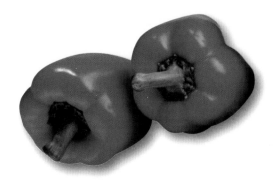

Spicy Shrimp

Ingredients

16oz/500g medium raw shrimp, peeled

⅔ cup lime juice

⅔ cup orange juice

1 hot pepper

1 clove garlic, minced

1 tsp brown sugar

1 red pepper

½ small red onion, sliced

2 tbsp coriander

2 ripe tomatoes, chopped

salt and black pepper

Method

To make the filling: heat the oil in a skillet. Sauté the onion until golden brown. Add the tomatoes and sauté 5 minutes.

Add the fish, the shrimp, the scallops, the peppers, the oregano and the lemon rasp and sauté 3-4 minutes until the seafood is done, while shaking the pan.

Spoon the filling into the middle of each tortilla and sprinkle with the feta.

Fold the tortillas closed and serve them immediately.

Ingredients

8 flour tortillas, heated

⅔ cup feta, crumbled

Seafood filling:

1 tsp vegetable oil; 1 onion, diced

2 tomatoes, cut; ¾ lb/375g white fish, in cubes

¾ lb/375g raw, medium-sized shrimp, peeled and deveined

3 medium-sized fresh green Spanish peppers, finely cut

2 tbsp fresh oregano, finely chopped

½ tsp grated lemon peel

12 scallops

Shrimp Tacos

Index